Tiny Warrior

A Preemie's Fight for Life

Nicholette Goffe

Acknowledgement

This book would not exist without the unwavering support of my family and friends who stood beside me during the darkest and most uncertain days of my life.

I am deeply grateful to the dedicated NICU nurses and doctors whose compassion and expertise cared for my daughter and countless others with such grace.

To my daughter, my tiny warrior, thank you for teaching me the true meaning of resilience and hope.

To every mother who has ever watched their child battle for life, and every family navigating the fragile journey of prematurity, this is for you. Your hope, your tears, and your prayers are valid and seen.

Nicholette

Dedication

To my Tiny Warrior,

You were born fighting, and you taught me what true strength looks like.

Every breath you took was a miracle. Every day you grew was a triumph.

This book is for you — my daughter, my light, my reason to believe in hope.

Author's Note

This book is a labor of love — a tribute to a tiny warrior whose strength and spirit have forever changed my life. It is a story of hope, fear, heartbreak, and triumph — a journey that many parents know all too well but few can truly understand until they have lived it.

This story is deeply personal. It is not fiction — it is our truth.

The photos shared throughout this book are moments frozen in time — raw, real, and sacred. They reflect joy, fear, exhaustion, and fierce love. Some were taken on days when I wasn't sure what tomorrow would bring. Others were captured in celebration, when we allowed ourselves to believe that our tiny warrior might just win this fight.

I share these images not for sympathy, but to honor the strength of one little girl who refused to give up, and the quiet resilience found in NICU parents everywhere.

I wrote this memoir not only to honor her fight for life but also to offer comfort and solidarity to every family navigating the fragile path of prematurity. If you are reading this, know that you are not alone.

Thank you for opening your heart to our story.

Table of Contents

CHAPTER 1
THE UNEXPECTED JOURNEY

It was supposed to be just a routine doctor's appointment, nothing out of the ordinary, or so I thought at the time. That morning, I had been experiencing some mild cramps. They weren't particularly intense, just a bit uncomfortable... more of a nagging sensation than anything truly painful. I chalked it up to the usual side effects of pregnancy and didn't think much of it.

I brought it up casually during my appointment, mentioning the cramps to my doctor. He reassured me with a calm smile, saying it was most likely just Braxton Hicks contractions or maybe even some normal ligament stretching, both common in pregnancy and usually nothing to worry about. His words were meant to be comforting, and at the moment, they were.

But as the hours passed, things began to change. The cramps didn't fade away as expected; instead, they gradually grew stronger. By the time midnight rolled around, the pain had escalated to something sharp and overwhelming, far beyond anything I had ever felt before. It was no longer just discomfort. It was real, searing pain.

Panicked and unsure of what was really going on, I called my sister. She listened carefully as I described what I was feeling and, without hesitation, told me I was likely in labor. Her voice was steady, but I could sense the urgency behind her words. She had been through this before and knew exactly what to look out for.

Without wasting another minute, we sprang into action. The hospital was nearly two hours away, a long drive under any circumstances, but especially daunting in the middle of the night while in pain.

I also called my doctor again, even though he was already on his way to Beijing for the 2016 Olympics. He answered quickly and told me to head straight to the hospital. There, the medical team would try their best to stop the contractions and delay the labor if possible.

Thankfully, my hospital bag had been packed in advance, something I had done weeks ago "just in case," not really believing I'd need it so soon. We grabbed it, made sure we had everything else we might need, and began our unexpected journey. The road ahead was uncertain, but one thing was clear... our lives were about to change.

CHAPTER 2
THE LONG DRIVE & THE BIRTH

The drive to the hospital felt like it stretched on forever. Every bump in the road seemed to amplify the contractions, each wave of pain more intense than the last. I clung desperately to the hope that once we arrived, the doctors would be able to intervene and somehow prevent an early delivery. I kept telling myself we still had time, that everything would slow down once we got there, but deep down, I knew things were moving too fast.

Her father, who was overseas at the time, stayed on the phone with my sister throughout the entire drive. His voice, though crackling through the distance, provided a small thread of comfort I didn't know I needed. I could barely speak; the pain was so overwhelming it stole my breath and my words. Still, I could hear him... his concern, his love, his helplessness. He stayed on the line, not saying much, but his presence was constant, and that meant everything.

By the time we finally arrived at the hospital, the situation had escalated far beyond what any of us had anticipated. Everything moved so quickly after that. I was immediately taken to a room, barely able to process what was happening. A doctor came in to examine me, and her expression changed the moment she checked. With a look of urgency, she told me I was already six centimeters dilated, well into active labor. I was stunned. I thought we had time, that this might just be a false alarm, but we were already past the point of slowing things down.

The doctor calmly but firmly explained that the baby would be coming very soon, and we needed to prepare for a preterm delivery. My mind raced with a thousand thoughts, but none of them formed clearly. I only heard fragments of what she said... words like *risk, complications, NICU*. My baby was coming too early, and we had no choice but to face what lay ahead.

The medical team sprang into action. They began preparing for what could be a complicated delivery. I remember hearing them mention the possible challenges, how babies born prematurely often struggle with breathing, feeding, and maintaining their body temperature. I heard the word *ventilator* and felt my heart clenched. It all felt surreal.

In a haze, I called my baby's father again to update him. My voice shook as I spoke, but I managed to explain what was happening. He was still trying to grasp the reality of it, just as I was. The moment neither of us had expected had arrived, and now we were both caught in its full force. Despite the distance, his voice gave me strength.

I also contacted a few close family members and friends. I didn't even know what to say at first, just that the baby was coming, and we needed prayers and support. One by one, they made their way to the hospital. Their presence was unplanned but deeply appreciated. As they began to arrive, I felt a wave of emotional relief wash over me. I wasn't alone in this. I was surrounded by people who loved me and who were ready to stand by my side through it all.

A few hours later, everything blurred into urgency. I was rushed into the delivery room, the bright lights and fast footsteps all blending together. At exactly 9:49 AM, our daughter was born. But there were no triumphant cries, no celebratory cheers. The room was eerily quiet, so quiet that it was almost too much to bear.

There was only the soft shuffle of nurses moving quickly, the rhythmic beeping of machines, and the heavy silence that filled every corner of the room. I held my breath. I had imagined this moment so many times, always picturing the joy of hearing her first cry, but that cry didn't come.

The silence felt deafening. My heart pounded in my chest as I looked toward the team working around her. I could barely see anything clearly through my tears and exhaustion. Then, one of the nurses looked at me. Her face softened, and she gave me the gentlest smile.

"She's here," she said quietly.

In that fragile, breathless moment, those two words shattered the silence. And though my daughter hadn't made a sound, my heart swelled with an indescribable mix of love, fear, and relief.

The medical team worked with precision and speed. They placed a small device in her mouth, administering oxygen, I assumed and prepared to move her to the Neonatal Intensive Care Unit (NICU). I couldn't stop watching her, couldn't stop wishing I could hold her, even for just a second.

Before they wheeled her away, someone turned to me and gently asked, "What is the sex of the baby?"

The question caught me off guard. I was still trembling, still in shock, my body aching and my mind struggling to catch up. Through the fog, I managed to whisper, "It's a girl."

And with those words, the whirlwind of the past several hours became real. She was here. My baby girl was here.

CHAPTER 3
THE UNEXPECTED CHALLENGE

Just as I began to process the overwhelming flood of emotions... the joy, the shock, the exhaustion, that came with our daughter's arrival, another unexpected challenge surfaced. I was still reeling from the whirlwind of her early birth when the medical team informed me that the placenta, which normally follows the baby shortly after delivery, had not fully come out. What should have been a routine part of the process, quickly turned into a growing concern.

Parts of the placenta were still inside and despite their careful efforts my body wasn't letting go. The medical staff worked patiently, trying to assist with its natural expulsion, but nothing changed. I could see their expressions growing more concerned, and that concern quickly became contagious. I began to feel the rising tension in the room, the weight of uncertainty settling over everything.

One of the doctors gently explained the risks to me. A retained placenta isn't something to take lightly; it can lead to serious complications like postpartum hemorrhaging, infection, and further trauma and would need to be removed manually. The words hit me hard. I had barely come to terms with my daughter's premature birth, and now I was being told I need a manual procedure to remove the retained placenta. The thought was terrifying, but there was no time to dwell on fear. This had to be done, and it had to be done quickly.

The room became a flurry of controlled urgency. The medical team moved swiftly, preparing for the procedure with practiced precision. The doctor assigned to perform the removal slipped on a long, wrist-length glove, her expression calm but focused. There was no time for small talk or reassurance; her quiet confidence had to be enough.

With steady hands, she carefully inserted her arm to locate and detach the remaining parts of placenta from the uterine wall. The sensation was indescribable; deep, invasive, and utterly overwhelming. I could feel every movement, every press and pull. It was uncomfortable in a way that made the pain of labor feel distant, almost manageable by comparison. This, somehow, felt even worse. Not just physically, but emotionally. The vulnerability, the fear, the sheer exhaustion, it all came crashing down on me at once.

I gripped the sides of the bed, holding my breath as the minutes stretched on. It felt like time had stopped, like the room had shrunk to the sound of my heartbeat and the doctor's quiet instructions. Finally, after what felt like an eternity, the doctor gave a nod. The retained placenta had been removed.

Relief flooded through my body, so strong it nearly brought me to tears. I hadn't realized just how tense I'd been until that very moment. Everything was finally over or at least, this part of the journey was. The worst had passed, and I was finally moved to the recovery room.

Physically, I was drained. Every part of me ached, and I felt as though I had been through a storm I hadn't prepared for. But beneath the exhaustion, there was something else… something deeper. I felt an immense, profound sense of gratitude. Gratitude for the medical team who had acted swiftly and skillfully, for the support of my loved ones, and for the fact that, against the odds, both my daughter and I had made it through.

This wasn't the birth story I had imagined… but it was ours. Raw, real, and unforgettable.

CHAPTER 4
THE NICU AND THE WAITING

I had not seen my daughter since the moment she was born, and the hours that followed were some of the most emotionally draining and uncertain I had ever experienced. I was bleeding heavily, and the medical staff remained focused on stabilizing me, making sure I was out of immediate danger. While I understood their priority, it left me with little to no information about my baby's condition. The separation from her was unbearable, every second apart felt like a piece of me was missing.I couldn't stop replaying the moment she was taken from the delivery room, so tiny, so fragile, surrounded by a flurry of unfamiliar faces and machines. My heart ached with questions. Was she okay? Was she scared? Was she warm enough? Did she know she wasn't alone? I longed to hold her, to cradle her in my arms, to let her hear my voice and feel my warmth, to show her that she was deeply loved and never alone. But all I could do in those long, empty hours was wait and wonder.

Time moved slowly, so slowly that each minute stretched on like an hour. I was engulfed in a fog of helplessness, guilt, and fear. Was I doing enough for her? Did she think I had abandoned her in her most vulnerable moment? I ached to be near her, to protect her, to be the mother I had imagined I would be.

Eventually, after what truly felt like an eternity, I was wheeled onto the recovery ward and placed on IV medications. I was still weak, but the thought of seeing my daughter was the only thing keeping me grounded. Family members and friends had gathered around my bed, offering their love and encouragement. Their presence was comforting, and for a brief moment, I felt surrounded by hope. They stayed with me for a while, trying to lift my spirits, speaking softly and reassuringly.

But when they left, a wave of isolation swept over me. I looked around the room and saw other mothers holding their newborns, soft coos and cries filling the space, warm skin against skin. Meanwhile, I remained alone. No cries. No baby. Just silence and the persistent uncertainty of my daughter's condition.

Desperate, I asked when I could see her. A nurse told me I would be allowed to visit her in the NICU once the IV medication had run its course. But I couldn't wait that long. The pull to be near her was too strong to ignore. With effort, I got out of the bed, my legs still shaky and grabbed the IV pole beside me. Step by step, I made my way down the hallway, the wheels of the pole clicking softly against the floor, each movement bringing me closer to her.

And then I saw her... my precious baby girl. She lay on an infant warmer, her tiny body connected to tubes and monitors, each machine blinking and beeping rhythmically. She had an indentation in her chest wall, it appeared like a small hole, and I was told it was related to the respiratory distress she experienced as a newborn. She looked so small, so delicate, yet somehow still full of life and strength. I moved closer and reached out with trembling fingers. As I gently touched her hand, she responded, her tiny fingers curled around mine. It was a small gesture, but it held so much meaning.

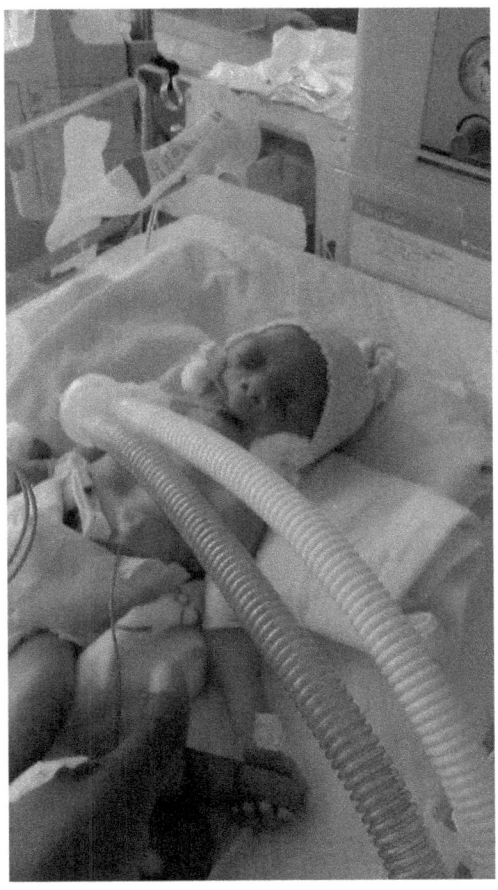

Her tiny fingers wrapped around mine, saying "I'm still fighting"

In that single, powerful moment, a wave of relief and emotion washed over me. She was alive. She was here. She was fighting. And I was here with her.

That moment changed everything. I realized this journey wasn't just about survival, it was about bonding, about resilience, about unwavering love. It was about finding strength in the most fragile of moments and holding on to hope even in the darkest hours.

Each new day brought its own set of challenges; some big, some small, but each also came with new victories. The medical team was incredible, their expertise matched only by their compassion. And while the road ahead was still uncertain, one thing became crystal clear: we were in this together. My daughter, so small yet so fierce, was showing me what it meant to fight and to love without limits.

CHAPTER 5
THE NICU JOURNEY

Our daughter spent a total of six months and eleven days in the Neonatal Intensive Care Unit (NICU), a period marked by unimaginable challenges, countless medical interventions, and moments of both heartbreak and hope. The first five months were particularly harrowing. During this time, she was frequently placed on a ventilator, unable to breathe on her own. Her tiny body fought tirelessly against the odds, day in and day out.

Each attempt by the medical team to wean her off the ventilator ended in disappointment. Her oxygen levels would dip dangerously low, and time after time, the doctors had to resort to manually ventilating her just to keep her alive. Those moments were terrifying. Every alarm, every flurry of activity around her bed, sent waves of fear through us. We lived in constant anticipation, never knowing when the next emergency would strike.

Then came a turning point. One day, a nurse heard what she thought was a baby crying coming from our daughter's direction. Curious and concerned, she checked and discovered that our little warrior had somehow managed to pull out her own breathing tube. It was an unexpected act of strength... an act that prompted the medical team to reassess her condition immediately. After careful evaluation, they made the bold decision to attempt weaning her from the ventilator. This pivotal moment marked a major step in her fight for survival, revealing just how strong-willed and determined she truly was.

But her fight didn't end there. She was constantly in battle mode, her tiny hands always reaching for the tubes and lines that tethered her to life. Eventually, the nurses had to gently strap her hands down, not to restrain her spirit, but to protect her fragile body. It was a delicate balance between keeping her safe and allowing her enough freedom to move, to stretch, to be a baby. Yet even then, she showed unyielding strength, reminding us every single day that she wasn't giving up.

The very next day, however, we were dealt a crushing blow. Just as we began to hope, her lungs collapsed. I remember it as if it happened yesterday. I walked into the NICU early that morning, eager to see her, only to find her warmer empty. My heart sank. Panic consumed me as I cried out, "Where is my baby?"

A doctor gently took me aside and brought me into his office. With a solemn expression, he explained that her lungs had collapsed overnight. She was being stabilized, he said, and they were preparing to surgically insert chest tubes to release the trapped air and allow her lungs to re-expand. I couldn't process it. My body shook. I could barely breathe. The wait that followed felt endless. I sat there, consumed by anxiety, silently pleading with God to protect her. The tears flowed freely. I couldn't stop them.

Eventually, a nurse informed me that she had been stabilized and I could see her. Walking into that room and seeing her again was a moment of overwhelming relief. There she was; alive, breathing, surviving. But the chest tubes in her tiny chest made it painfully clear just how fragile her condition still was. My heart ached. As I approached her, I noticed tears slowly leaking from her closed eyes. It shattered me. I broke down, imagining the pain she must have been in, the discomfort, the fear she couldn't express.

I longed to scoop her up, hold her close, tell her she was safe, but I couldn't. The tubes, the wires, the machines, all of it kept me at a distance. It was one of the most helpless feelings I've ever experienced. That moment, that image of her lying there with silent tears, is burned into my memory. It was a stark reminder of how fine the line was between strength and fragility, between life and loss. It was bittersweet, being so close to her, yet unable to comfort her in the way a mother should.

Another significant part of her NICU journey was the need for frequent blood transfusions. In total, she received 14 transfusions, each one given to replenish what she had lost due to internal or external hemorrhaging and to ensure her body could carry oxygen efficiently. With every transfusion, we held our breath, praying for no negative reactions. Thankfully, she handled each one with quiet strength, and the medical team monitored her closely, making adjustments to her care to support her delicate recovery.

Feeding her was another uphill battle. Her digestive system was severely underdeveloped. She couldn't tolerate even small amounts of milk or nutrients. Every time the nurses tried to feed her, she would bring it back up, her body simply couldn't keep anything down. As days passed without adequate nutrition, she began to develop severe edema. Her tiny body became so swollen, she looked like an inflated balloon- her delicate feature nearly unrecognizable. The swelling was so extreme that her neck disappeared into the puffiness, making it look like her head was resting directly on her chest. The doctors suspected Malnutrition, due to her inability to process the feeds. This constant cycle, start a feed, watch her, stop the feed, wait, and try again... was exhausting. Physically, emotionally, mentally... for all of us.

Not long after that, we faced another big decision, the surgery. Doctors recommended inserting a tube through her groin up toward her heart to feed her. She wasn't processing food, and they believed this would help. But the risks terrified me.

I went home and talked it over with her father. For two days, we discussed, cried, went back and forth trying to make the right decision. I kept saying, "I don't want to do this. I don't know what to do." We were torn. Completely torn. That night, I told myself, If I wake up tomorrow and feel peace, I'll agree to it. But when I woke up, that peace wasn't there. Just anxiety. Fear. Doubt.

Still unsure, I went to the hospital and spoke with the surgery doctor. She laid everything out, what the procedure involved, what could go wrong. And in that moment, I knew. I couldn't do it. I had to trust my instincts. The risks felt too high. The fear in my chest was too loud to ignore. I made the decision. I told them no.

The doctor wasn't happy. I could see it on her face. But I had to stand my ground. I had to make the choice I believed was best for my daughter. It wasn't easy, but it was mine to make and I made it with my whole heart.

It was at this moment that a new consultant who just joined her care team came on board. She immediately took charge with compassion and determination, collaborating closely with the NICU doctors, nutritionist, and pharmacist to address the swelling. Together they worked tirelessly to adjust her nutrition, medications, and care plan. It was the first time in weeks we had felt a glimmer of hope, knowing that someone was fighting as hard for her as we were. Within a few days the swelling started to subside, and she was looking like her normal self again. Seeing this gave me confirmation that I made the right decision about the surgery.

On top of all this, she had a team of specialists watching her every move. A cardiologist monitored her heart, a neurologist examined her brain activity and development, and a nutritionist crafted delicate plans to give her the nutrients she desperately needed. Physical therapists helped her stretch and strengthen, while respiratory therapists ensured her lungs received every bit of support possible. It felt like there was a new concern every day, a new treatment to try, a new hurdle to overcome.

Still, even in the darkest moments, glimmers of hope would break through. Every day that she survived, every tiny improvement, whether a better oxygen reading or a small gain in weight, was worth celebrating. These weren't just medical milestones; they were victories. Hard-earned, soul-stirring victories that spoke volumes about her will to live and the dedication of the doctors and nurses who never gave up on her.

And then, there was the moment that changed everything for me... the first time I held her.

I'll never forget it. I don't think words will ever truly do it justice. It was about two months after she was born. Until then, I had only seen her on the warmer, surrounded by tubes and wires, too fragile to hold. That day, a nurse gently removed some of her tubes and placed her in my arms for a shared hold. That was the first time I really, truly held her.

She was so light. Her skin looked almost translucent, so pale it didn't seem real. I remember thinking she might just slip away if I held her too tightly or not tightly enough. I felt joy, yes, but also an ache I can't describe. A kind of beautiful sadness, one only a mother in a NICU can understand. I hadn't even properly seen her right after birth, not like a mother should, and maybe I've said that before, but I'll say it again, because that kind of moment never leaves you.

And then there was the fear that never left me: the fear of every call. Every time the hospital number flashed on my screen, my heart dropped. Whether I was down the hall in the parent room or just stepped out for a moment, that ring filled me with dread. I asked the nurses, "Please don't call me for every little thing. Just do what you have to." I even joked about it, calling it my "sign," but deep down, every call was a potential storm.

It got to the point where my body couldn't take it anymore. One evening, around 5.30 pm I started feeling dizzy and weak, I looked up and saw my brother walked into the parent room, just like he did every day. I saw him, smiled… and then everything went black. I passed out. When I came to, it was 7 p.m. I had no memory of what happened. My body had reached its limit… from the exhaustion, the stress, the constant fear.

I didn't have postpartum depression, not in the way people usually talk about it. What I had was something else. Anxiety. Maybe even trauma. My mind and body were in overdrive, always on alert, always worrying, always afraid of the next emergency.

CHAPTER 6
THE SEIZURE CRISIS

The days in the NICU had become a relentless tide of endless waiting and whispered prayers, a fragile dance between hope and fear. I had grown accustomed to the sterile hum of machines and the steady beep that marked every breath she took. But no amount of preparation could brace me for the moment the nurse found me just as I stepped away from my daughter's bedside.

Her face was somber, the kind of expression that carries news heavy enough to silence a room. "The doctors need to speak with you," she said softly, almost hesitating, as if trying to soften the blow before it landed.

My heart stopped. Suddenly, the world felt impossibly small, as if the very air was squeezed out of the room. I followed her, footsteps uncertain, barely able to breathe. In the small consultation room, a group of doctors sat waiting; silent, eyes serious, faces unreadable like a storm about to break. The lead doctor gestured to a chair, and I sat down, legs trembling, trying to steady myself.

"We've been monitoring your daughter closely," she began, her voice calm but heavy, "and she has started having seizures."

Those words landed like a cruel, jagged blow, piercing, unexpected. I swallowed hard, my throat tightening. Seizures... I had only ever seen them in films, like distant nightmares that belonged to someone else's story. Never did I imagine they would invade mine, or that they would invade my baby's fragile body.

"What does this mean?" I asked, voice cracking, barely a whisper.

The doctor's eyes softened, but her words remained grave. "It means her condition has worsened. Seizures in newborns are often a sign of serious neurological distress. We're doing everything possible, but you must be prepared... there is a risk she might not survive."

The room seemed to tilt and spin, the walls closing in like shadows swallowing the light. My breath hitched. I wanted to scream, demand that they fix this, that they take it back, that they erase the word 'seizure' from her body, from this cruel world.

But I was silent. I only nodded. Tears fell unchecked, tracing cold paths down my cheeks as a hollow ache filled my chest.

When I left the room, the fog of shock clung to me. My mind raced with unanswerable questions: Will she survive? What kind of life awaits her? How will I carry this unbearable weight if she doesn't?

I returned to her bedside, where her tiny, vulnerable body lay beneath the gentle warmth of the machine lights. I reached out and took her hand; so small, so delicate and whispered words of love, of hope, desperate for her to hear me, to feel me even in her silence.

The days that followed blurred into one another, each a relentless tide of tests, medication adjustments, and sleepless vigils. The NICU became both prison and sanctuary, a place where hope hung by the thinnest thread, yet where every small breath, every flutter of her lashes, was a miracle fought for fiercely.

I sat beside her every day, watching her chest rise and fall, my fingers tracing the faint warmth of her skin through the thin blankets. I whispered to her stories of the world she was born into, a world I wanted her to live in fully, no matter what. I told her about the sun and the stars, about the laughter waiting for her, about the love that surrounded her even now. I spoke through my tears, hoping the sound of my voice could bridge the vast silence that illness had brought.

There were moments when the machines screamed warnings, and nurses rushed in a flurry of urgent motions. My heart shattered a little more each time. But in the quiet that followed, when she lay still again, I found a fragile strength I never knew I had... holding onto every breath, every tiny sign of life.

Slowly, ever so painfully slow, the seizures began to ebb. The doctors grew cautiously hopeful, their tired eyes lighting up behind masks of professionalism. But I dared not let myself believe too fully. I learned to live in that fragile space, between hope and fear because hope, when it felt so fragile, was a fierce rebellion against despair.

And then, one day, it happened.

Her eyes fluttered open. Not just a blink, but a steady, searching gaze that met mine directly. It was as if she was reaching through the darkness, pulling me back from the edge of hopelessness. In that moment, all the exhaustion, all the tears, all the fear... everything, felt worth it. The tiny spark of life in her gaze was the brightest light I had ever seen.

I leaned closer, my voice barely a breath, "You're going to be okay, my love. You have to be."

And as she looked at me, with the faintest flutter of a smile, I knew deep in my soul, she was fighting to stay, to live, to grow. And I would be there with her, every step of the way.

Her eyes met mine, we were in this together

CHAPTER 7
GOD'S PRESENCE IN THE NICU

In the cold, sterile halls of the NICU, under the harsh glow of fluorescent lights, the world felt suspended in a fragile, almost sacred stillness. Machines beeped steadily, nurses moved swiftly but quietly, and parents like me lingered near incubators and warmers, caught between hope and heartbreak. It was a place where time lost its usual meaning, a place where seconds stretched and minutes blurred, each moment charged with a weight impossible to describe.

When my daughter was admitted, she was just one among a group of babies who had arrived in those tense early hours, tiny lives fighting their own battles, each cradled in the arms of hope. There were about seven parents in that shared space, each of us clinging to the fragile thread of our newborns' breaths. Among those babies was a set of twins, brought in with hope and fear twined tightly together.

Over the following days and weeks, I watched the heartbreak unfold. One by one, those precious babies passed away. The nurses moved between incubators like silent angels, offering what comfort they could, but the truth was unyielding and cruel. The loss around us was overwhelming.

By the time the weekend came, the mother of the twins had lost one of her babies. It was a quiet, devastating blow… one twin gone, one left alone. And among all the babies who had come in at the same time, it was down to just two: her remaining twin and my daughter. Two small, fragile lives holding on, the last flickers of hope from a night filled with so much sorrow.

One particular night is forever etched into my memory. The NICU had become a world apart from the one I had known, one where doctors gathered around these two tiny souls with urgency and exhaustion. Her baby, the last twin, was surrounded by a team of doctors. My baby, too, had a group of doctors hovering, their faces grim, their hands moving with urgent purpose.

The two mothers, strangers until then, found ourselves drawn together in a shared vigil. We spoke quietly, offering each other strength we barely felt ourselves. The corridors echoed with the sound of medical staff calling for blood, moving quickly, the tension almost palpable. We prayed together in that small room — words of hope and desperation flowing from our lips like a sacred lifeline.

But the night held its own fate. As dawn crept closer, the news came, her baby had passed.

The weight of that moment crushed me. I couldn't imagine the depth of her pain, having just lost one child, now losing the other. My heart ached for her, for the unimaginable grief that would follow. And yet, in that same dark moment, my daughter still clung to life.

Her name, chosen by her father before she was even born, means "from heaven" and "fulfilled." At the time, we hadn't grasped the weight those meanings would carry. But in that moment, watching her cling to life while others slipped away, it felt as if her name had always been a promise. It was as if God Himself had laid His hand upon her, steadying her through the storm. She was heavenly, yes, but she was also ful-filled- complete in her will to live, in her quiet strength. It was as though her name had been chosen not by us, but for her, long before we even met her

I carried the weight of the night with me. I thought about the mother who had lost her twins; how she must be burying a part of her soul. I remembered the faces of the other parents whose babies had passed, whose lives were forever marked by those empty incu-bators and silent monitors. And I thought about my daughter, the one who had survived.

There was a strange kind of bond among us, par-ents who had come in as strangers but were bound by the sharp edges of loss and hope. We had built a fragile community in the NICU, united in the quiet hours and the whispered prayers. We watched each other's backs, shared tears, and clung to the smallest signs of progress.

Even now, I hesitate to speak of the losses in detail because it is not my story to tell. But my daughter's survival is forever intertwined with that shared experience, with the strength found in a room full of grieving parents and vigilant doctors. I saw the fragility of life up close and the divine presence that seemed to linger in those halls, offering a quiet promise that we were not alone.

In the darkest moments, when hope felt threadbare, I felt God's hand upon us. It was in the silent prayers we whispered, in the way strangers became a family, in the quiet strength of mothers and fathers holding their babies close despite the odds.

I often wonder how I found the strength to keep going, to hope, to pray, to believe. But in those nights of uncertainty, it was faith that carried me through. Faith that my daughter was held by something greater than all our fears.

And so, as I sat alone one evening in the empty parent lounge, surrounded by empty chairs that told stories of love and loss, I felt a profound sense of peace. God was present in that place, in that pain, and in that hope. And I knew, with a certainty deeper than words, that with His grace, my daughter would continue to fight, and I would be there to hold her hand every step of the way.

CHAPTER 8
THE JOURNEY OF A FIRST-TIME MOTHER

Becoming a mother for the first time is a journey unlike any other, a passage filled with anticipation, excitement, and the kind of joy that feels both overwhelming and sacred. But for me, that journey began not with the usual calm and celebration, but with a sudden rush of fear and uncertainty when our daughter arrived far earlier than we ever expected, at just twenty-seven weeks.

The moment I held her, even from a distance, my heart shattered and soared all at once. Her body was so small, so fragile, a delicate promise lying there in nothing but a diaper far too big for her tiny frame. Her tiny hands, no bigger than my thumb, clenched and unclenched with a life force that refused to be dimmed. Each little breath she took was a miracle, a defiance against the odds stacked against her.

As a first-time mother, I found myself navigating uncharted waters. I had never imagined the rollercoaster of emotions that would flood me, joy at her every small movement, terror at every beep of the monitor, hope tethered tightly to fear. In the sterile, humming environment of the NICU, love alone was never enough. I quickly realized that being her mother meant becoming more than just a nurturer; it meant becoming her fiercest advocate.

I learned to speak up in the face of uncertainty, to ask questions even when my voice trembled with exhaustion and grief. I had to trust the skilled hands and knowledge of the doctors and nurses, yet hold tightly to my own instincts as a mother who knew her child better than anyone else. It was a delicate balance, between surrender and fight, that I had never been prepared for.

The nights were the hardest. When the hospital corridors emptied and the world outside seemed to slow, I found myself alone in the parent lounge, tears often spilling down my face as I struggled with the weight of doubt. Was I strong enough? Was I doing everything I could for my daughter? The loneliness was crushing at times, the silence echoing with questions that had no easy answers.

But even separated by continents, my spouse's presence was a lifeline. Through late-night video calls, his calm voice reached across the miles, wrapping me in warmth and reassurance. Though he could not be there physically, his faith in our daughter's strength and in me as her mother never wavered. His quiet confidence was a comfort to my weary heart, a reminder that we were in this together, united by love and determination, no matter the distance.

Each time I returned to my daughter's bedside, watching her chest rise and fall with each fragile breath, I found a renewed sense of purpose. She was fighting, and so was I… for her, for us, for the life that stretched before us like an uncertain horizon. It was a journey I had never anticipated but one I embraced with everything I had.

Beyond the sterile walls of the NICU, the presence of family and friends became my lifeline — a beacon of light piercing through the darkest, most suffocating moments. When I was overwhelmed by exhaustion that threatened to swallow me whole, it was their calls, their messages, their visits that lifted my spirit and reminded me I was not alone. Each word of encouragement, each whispered prayer, and every shared tear made me feel held, as if the love and strength I needed were being sent to me on invisible wings.

They were my connection to the world beyond those hospital corridors — reminding me that my daughter was not just lying there on the infant warmer, fighting for her life, but that she was also cradled in the hearts of so many who wished for her survival and thriving. Their faith in her, and in me, was an invisible but powerful force that steadied me when my own courage faltered. Even when my body screamed for rest and my mind swirled with fear, I could feel their love wrapped around me like a warm, unbreakable shield.

But beneath all the comfort and kindness, I carried a truth that was raw and unvarnished: this journey was as much about endurance as it was about love. Motherhood, especially when thrust upon you in such fragile, uncertain circumstances, reveals parts of yourself you never knew existed. It strips away all illusions of control and perfection, leaving you exposed to the depths of your own vulnerability. And yet, within that vulnerability, I found a well of strength I didn't know I had.

I learned that strength is not always loud or visible, it is the quiet persistence of showing up, day after day, even when your heart feels shattered into a thousand pieces. It is the courage to face each new day without knowing what the outcome will be, to keep hoping even when hope feels like the most fragile thread. It is the grace to accept help when you need it, to lean on others without shame, and to understand that vulnerability is not weakness but a vital part of this journey.

In those long, lonely hours at the hospital, when the world outside seemed to be moving on without me, I learned to cherish the smallest victories. A tiny grasp of my finger, a flutter of her eyelids, a moment of steady breathing. These fragile moments were like sparks of light in the darkness, reminders that life, no matter how delicate, is fierce and beautiful. Each little sign of progress became a reason to keep going, to keep believing in a future that sometimes felt so far away.

Sometimes, when I watched her sleeping face bathed in the soft glow of the monitors, I felt overwhelmed by the depth of my love for her, a love so profound it scared me. It was a love that transcended fear and doubt, a love that refused to give up even when I felt utterly powerless. That love was my anchor, the force that held me steady through every storm.

Looking back now, I can see how this journey shaped me, not just as a mother, but as a human being.

It taught me what unconditional love truly means, the kind of love that does not ask for anything in return, that endures beyond pain and uncertainty. It showed me the power of faith, not always in a religious sense, but faith in life, in healing, and in the incredible resilience of the human spirit. And it revealed the remarkable strength that lies within a mother's heart, a strength forged in the crucible of fear, hope, and relentless devotion.

Through every tear shed in the quiet hours, every sleepless night spent watching over her, and every whispered prayer sent into the unknown, I discovered that motherhood is more than a role or a title. It is a journey of the soul, woven with threads of love, courage, and endless grace. It is about learning to be present in both the joy and the pain, to embrace the unpredictability of life, and to hold onto hope even when the path is unclear.

Now, as I watch my daughter grow, stronger and more vibrant with each passing day... I carry the memory of those early, fragile moments close to my heart. The days of fear and trembling hope, the nights filled with prayer and silent tears, the times when the future seemed so uncertain. Those memories remind me of how far we have come, and how fierce and unyielding a mother's love can be.

That love, unwavering and fierce, will forever guide me on this beautiful, unpredictable journey called motherhood. It is a love that has taught me to cherish every breath, every smile, every heartbeat, knowing that each one is a gift. And it is a love that has given me the strength to face whatever challenges lie ahead, with faith that no matter what, we will endure.

Motherhood, I have learned, is not about perfection. It's not about having all the answers or never feeling afraid. It's about showing up, again and again, with an open heart, ready to give your all, no matter the cost. And in that giving, in that relentless devotion, lies the true miracle of this journey.

CHAPTER 9
VALENTINE DAY MIRACLE

February 14, 2017 — a date forever etched in my heart. It was not just Valentine's Day; it was the day our daughter came home from the NICU, after spending six long months and eleven days in a relentless fight for life. That Tuesday morning in Kingston, Jamaica, the sun shone warmly, the air carried a soft breeze, and the temperature reached a comfortable 28°C (82°F). The world outside felt alive, gentle, and full of promise, a stark contrast to the sterile, cold nights we had endured inside the hospital's neonatal intensive care unit.

I remember the silence of that morning, punctuated only by the quiet hum of the car engine and the faint rustle of leaves outside. In my arms, I cradled the tiny, fragile life that had been our entire world for so many months. She was so small; a delicate miracle whose every breath felt like a triumph. But as I looked down, I saw the evidence of her battle etched upon her body.

Her hands and feet, once so impossibly tiny, bore the faint scars left by countless IV insertions, patches of hardened skin, subtle discolorations where the nurses and doctors had struggled to nourish and heal her. Those marks told a story of pain, endurance, and relentless care. I traced my fingers gently over the smooth skin on her head, now completely bald, a necessity forced upon us by the medical team to allow easier access to veins on her scalp for IV lines. It was heartbreaking to see the tiny dome of her head, once perfectly round, now bearing a slight flattening at the back, a gentle slope formed by months spent lying on the infant warmer that kept her alive.

There were other, more subtle reminders: the faint indentation around her mouth left by the ventilator tube that had supported her fragile breaths for most of her stay. These were not just scars but the silent testimony of a life sustained by science, care, and sheer willpower. Every mark was a chapter in her story, a story of survival, of strength, and of the countless hours she had spent fighting against all odds.

Around us, the hospital staff had gathered. Faces that had become familiar over these months — doctors who had saved her life more than once, nurses who had comforted her in the darkest hours — now beamed with pride and relief. A nurse who had been our steadfast companion throughout the ordeal stepped forward, her eyes warm with emotion. Looking tenderly at our tiny girl, she whispered, "She's a miracle."

That single word, spoken with such quiet reverence, struck a chord deep within me. In the sterile, clinical world of the NICU, where life and death hung in precarious balance, to be called a "miracle" was more than a label; it was a sacred blessing. It acknowledged the impossible, a child who had faced death and had emerged alive, a beacon of hope amid despair.

As I held her close, I felt an overwhelming mixture of emotions, gratitude, awe, relief, and an almost unbearable joy. She was no longer just the fragile infant hooked up to machines and monitors; she was our daughter, our fierce little warrior who had fought with everything she had and won. In that moment, I realized that she was more than a medical triumph, she was the living embodiment of resilience, hope, and love.

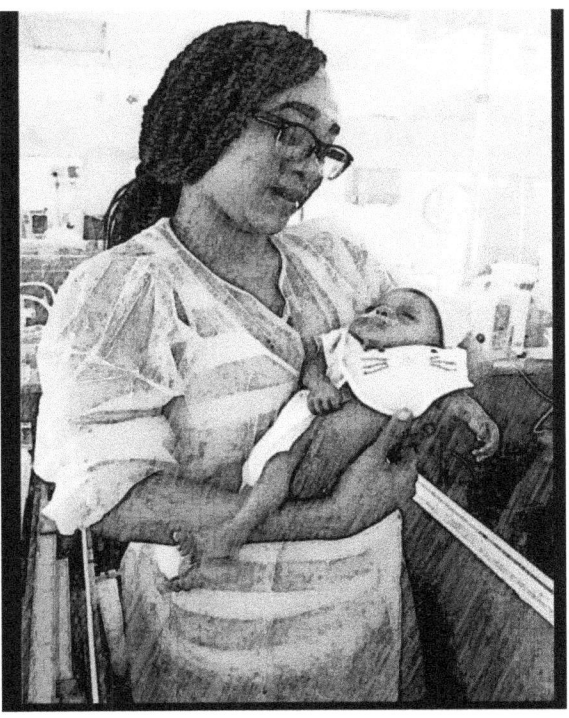

After 195 days in the NICU, our little warrior is finally coming home.

Driving home that day, I couldn't help but reflect on the long and painful journey that had brought us here. I thought of the countless hours spent by her side in the NICU, watching monitors and hoping for steady heartbeats, breathing patterns, and weight gain. I remembered the nights filled with whispered prayers, spoken in trembling voices or silent tears, the constant anxiety gnawing at my heart. And I thought about the unwavering support of family and friends; their calls, messages, and visits that reminded me we were not alone in this fight.

Even though the road was grueling, every second had been worth it. Our daughter had shown a strength that surpassed anything I'd ever known. Her tiny body had endured tubes, needles, ventilators, and medications, yet her spirit remained unbroken. She was fighting not just for herself but for all of us, for every parent who had ever sat helplessly beside an incubator, wishing for a miracle.

That day, Valentine's Day took on a meaning I had never anticipated. It wasn't about flowers, chocolates, or romantic gestures. It was about love in its rawest, most powerful form. The love of a mother who had watched her child battle for survival and had never once given up hope. The love of a family bound together by faith, endurance, and unwavering support. The love that, despite every hardship, refused to let go.

Pulling into our driveway, I felt a deep sense of peace settle over me. Our daughter was finally home. Safe. Loved. Ours. The weight of the months of fear and uncertainty lifted, replaced by a quiet joy and gratitude that filled every corner of my heart.

As I carried her inside, I whispered softly to her, promising to protect her, to cherish every moment, and to honor the incredible journey that had brought her to us. Each scar, each mark on her body was a testament not just to survival, but to the fierce, unbreakable bond between a mother and her child.

That Valentine's Day, amidst all the love that filled the air, I knew our daughter was the greatest gift of all, a true miracle in every sense of the word.

CHAPTER 10
THE BATTLE CONTINUED

Bringing our daughter home at last was a moment filled with indescribable joy and relief, a milestone that felt like the closing of a long and painful chapter. The months leading up to that day had been a relentless storm of fear and hope, and finally crossing the threshold into our home with her tiny body in our arms was like stepping into a fragile dream. The house, once just walls and furniture, became a sanctuary charged with new meaning. Every corner held a promise of healing and new beginnings.

Yet, deep down, beneath the surface of that joy, there lingered a quiet, unspoken fear. The fragile hope we carried was tempered by the reality of her tiny, vulnerable body, still so delicate from her premature arrival, still so incomplete. It was as if we were walking a tightrope, balancing between celebration and caution, between relief and dread. Every breath she took felt like a precious gift; every smile, a victory against the odds.

Exactly one month after that blessed day, the nightmare returned like a shadow creeping over the horizon. Our daughter was re-admitted to the hospital with pneumonia. The news hit us like a physical blow—cruel and unyielding. It felt like a cruel twist of fate, a merciless reminder that her premature birth had left her lungs underdeveloped and fragile, far more susceptible to infections than other children her age. The doctors explained with gentle but grave tones that her respiratory system was not yet ready to withstand the rigors of the outside world. The words "pneumonia" and "hospital readmission" echoed in our ears, filling us with an ache we had hoped never to know again.

Those six weeks back in the hospital were some of the darkest and most exhausting of our lives. The sterile walls of the ward became both a refuge and a prison, a place where hope and fear lived side by side. Night after night, I sat beside her crib, watching her chest rise and fall in shallow, fragile breaths. Her skin, pale and translucent under the harsh fluorescent lights, seemed so vulnerable. I held her tiny hand, smaller than my thumb, and prayed fiercely, prayers whispered into the quiet hum of machines and the occasional murmur of nurses. Every cough wracked her small frame, a cruel reminder of her struggle; each labored breath was a battle she was not guaranteed to win.

Sleep became a distant memory. Days and nights blurred into one endless vigil. The steady beeping of monitors punctuated the silence, each sound a reminder that she was still fighting. My heart clenched every time her oxygen saturation dipped or her breathing grew shallow. I learned to read the monitors like a language, the rise and fall of numbers telling a story of fragile hope and looming peril.

Despite the crushing weight of despair, she fought with a tenacity that left me breathless. It was impossible not to marvel at her courage, the fierce will beating within her tiny body. Day by day, her strength returned in small but undeniable increments. Slowly, the color came back to her cheeks, her eyes regained their bright spark, and her breaths grew steadier. It was a battle of endurance — not just hers, but ours as well. Watching her struggle and recover taught me the true meaning of resilience and courage in the face of overwhelming odds, a lesson seared into my soul.

When she was finally discharged again, it was with a new reality, she would come home on oxygen therapy. A tiny nasal cannula, a small but powerful lifeline, delivered a steady flow of oxygen into her nostrils. This thin tube became a permanent fixture in our lives, a symbol both of fragility and of hope. It tethered her to the equipment, reminding us of how precious and tenuous every breath truly was, yet it also granted her a kind of freedom, to move around, to explore, to grow in the familiar embrace of home. We cherished this deeply, grateful for every inch of progress.

The doctors explained that she had developed chronic lung disease (CLD), a condition common in premature infants whose lungs have not fully matured. The long-term oxygen therapy was essential, not just to keep her safe, but to support her growth and development, to shield her from further complications like pulmonary hypertension, and to help us bring her home sooner. The goal was to nurture her in the comfort of her own environment, surrounded by love and family, even as she continued to fight for every breath. It was a delicate balance between medical vigilance and the deep human need for warmth and normalcy.

At home, caring for her became a delicate dance of vigilance and love. Every day, we monitored her oxygen levels, watching the machines with careful eyes and adjusting the flow with precision. We learned the rhythms and nuances of the equipment—the subtle noises, the gentle hum, the blinking lights, each a vital part of the silent conversation between technology and life. The nasal cannula was more than just a tube; it was a lifeline, a symbol of the fragile thread on which her life now hung.

Our days were punctuated by moments of fear and joy, fear when the alarms sounded or when she seemed to struggle, joy in the quiet moments when she smiled, when she reached out her tiny fingers to hold ours. The house, once quiet and still, now echoed with the sounds of machines mingled with her soft breathing and occasional coos. We became experts in the art of gentle care, the language of soft touches and whispered reassurances. We learned to read her needs beyond words, to sense her discomfort, her fatigue, her small triumphs.

Though tethered to the equipment, she was still our daughter; full of life, curiosity, and the stubborn spark of will that no illness could dim. Every day with her was a gift, every breath a victory. We held on tightly to hope, knowing that this battle was far from over, but also that it was not without moments of grace and beauty. In those long, fragile days, we discovered the true depths of love, how it could carry us through the darkest nights, and how it could transform fear into fierce determination.

Yet, amidst the constant care and worry, life continued to happen. We celebrated the small victories with the joy of parents witnessing miracles: her first smile, a fleeting curve of lips that melted our hearts; her first wobbly steps, unsteady but determined; her first words, fragile sounds that spoke volumes of her spirit. Every milestone was a triumph not only of survival but of a love that refused to be broken.

The long hours spent at home with oxygen equipment became woven into the fabric of our daily lives. Friends and family became part of our village, offering support and encouragement that buoyed our spirits. We learned to adapt, to become experts in medical care and fierce advocates for our daughter's needs. Each day brought new challenges, but also new moments of grace.

Through it all, I discovered depths of strength within myself I never knew existed. Motherhood had transformed into a relentless journey; one that demanded endurance, patience, and unwavering faith. It wasn't about perfection; it was about presence. It was about showing up every day, no matter how exhausted or afraid I felt, and loving our daughter fiercely.

Her struggle with chronic lung disease taught me that resilience is not just a trait but a way of being, a quiet determination to keep moving forward even when the path is uncertain. Our family grew stronger in ways we never imagined, bound together by shared hope, endless prayers, and the fierce protective love we held for our little girl.

Looking back, this chapter of our lives was as much about survival as it was about growth, both hers and ours. It was about navigating the complexities of parenthood under extraordinary circumstances and learning to find light even in the darkest moments.

Our daughter's fight continued, but so did our commitment to her, to love her without condition, to stand by her side through every challenge, and to celebrate every breath she took. Because in the midst of struggle, we found an unbreakable bond, a family shaped by courage, faith, and the beautiful, unpredictable journey of life.

CHAPTER 11
A Beacon of Hope

Throughout our NICU journey, we encountered a dedicated team of doctors, nurses, and specialists whose expertise and compassion were invaluable. Each played a crucial role in our daughter's care, providing comfort and guidance during an incredibly challenging time.

Among them, one consultant stood out—not just for her medical proficiency but for her steadfast support and empathy. From the moment she entered our lives, she became more than a healthcare provider; she became a source of strength and reassurance. This physician went above and beyond, ensuring that every aspect of our daughter's treatment was meticulously planned and executed.

I will never forget the calm in her voice as she explained complex procedures, the warmth in her presence as she comforted our anxious hearts, and the dedication she showed in ensuring our daughter's well-being. She didn't just treat a patient; She cared for a family.

Equally remarkable was a nurse whose presence brought a sense of calm amidst the chaos. With unflinching dedication, she tended to our daughter with a gentle touch and a kind word, making us feel seen and heard during every moment of uncertainty.

Together, they exemplified the profound impact of compassionate care, reminding us that amid medical uncertainty, humanity and kindness are powerful forces for healing.

Even after her discharge, the commitment didn't end. Our consultant doctor continued to monitor her progress, coordinating with other specialists and adjusting her care plan as needed. This ongoing support was invaluable, providing us with a sense of security and confidence as we navigated the challenges of caring for a child with complex medical needs.

The continuity of care provided by our consultant doctor exemplified the importance of building long-term relationships in healthcare. It wasn't just about treating an illness; it was about understanding our daughter's unique needs and advocating for her well-being at every stage of her development.

As parents, we are deeply grateful for the dedication and compassion shown by this physician. Her involvement was instrumental in our daughter's journey, and the impact will be felt for a lifetime.

CHAPTER 12
A Journey of Resilience and Love

As I sit here, reflecting on the path we've traveled, I am overwhelmed with gratitude and awe. From the moment our daughter was born 13 weeks early, weighing 1.29 kg, to the day she finally came home, our lives have been a testament to resilience, hope, and the unbreakable bond of love.

The NICU was a world of its own — sterile, intimidating, and filled with uncertainty. Yet, it was also a place where miracles happened daily. Our daughter was one of those miracles. She fought, she thrived, and she taught us the true meaning of strength.

Bringing her home was a moment of indescribable joy. But the journey didn't end there. We faced challenges, setbacks, and moments of doubt. Yet, with each obstacle, we found new depths of courage and determination. We learned to navigate the complexities of her care, to advocate for her needs, and to celebrate every small victory.

Through it all, we were not alone. Our family, friends, other parents, and the medical team stood by us, offering support, encouragement, and love. Their unshakable faith in our daughter fueled our own.

Looking back, I realize that this journey has been about more than just medical procedures and hospital stays. It's about discovering the power of hope, the importance of community, and the boundless capacity of a mother and father's love, as well as strong family support.

Our daughter is now thriving, a vibrant testament to the strength of the human spirit. And as I watch her grow, I am reminded daily of the miracles that surround us.

To anyone reading this who is facing their own journey, know this: you are not alone. There is strength within you, and there is hope. Keep fighting, keep believing, and know that love will guide you through.

Medical Disclaimer:

This book contains personal reflections and experiences related to medical care in a Neonatal Intensive Care Unit (NICU). It is not intended to provide medical advice or serve as a substitute for professional diagnosis, treatment, or guidance.

Please consult your doctor or medical provider regarding any health concerns or decisions.

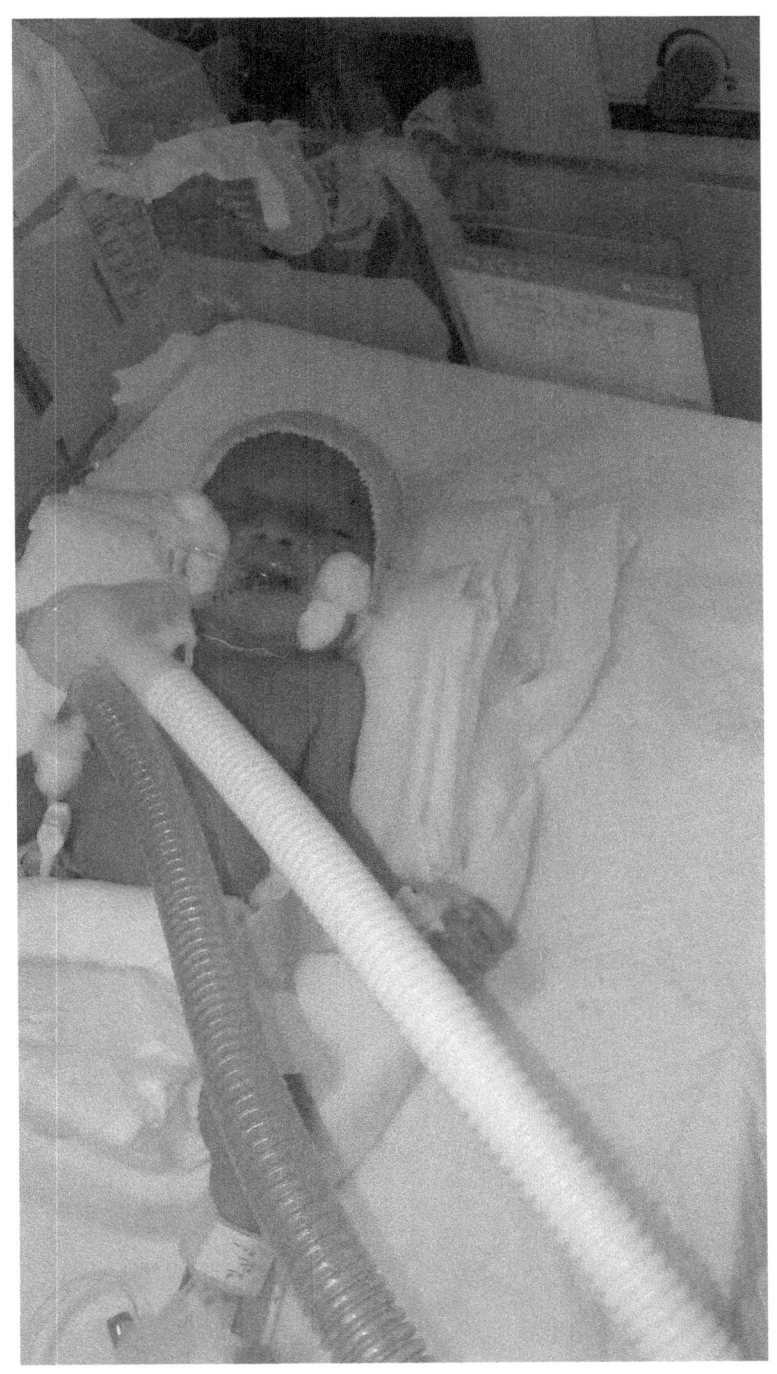

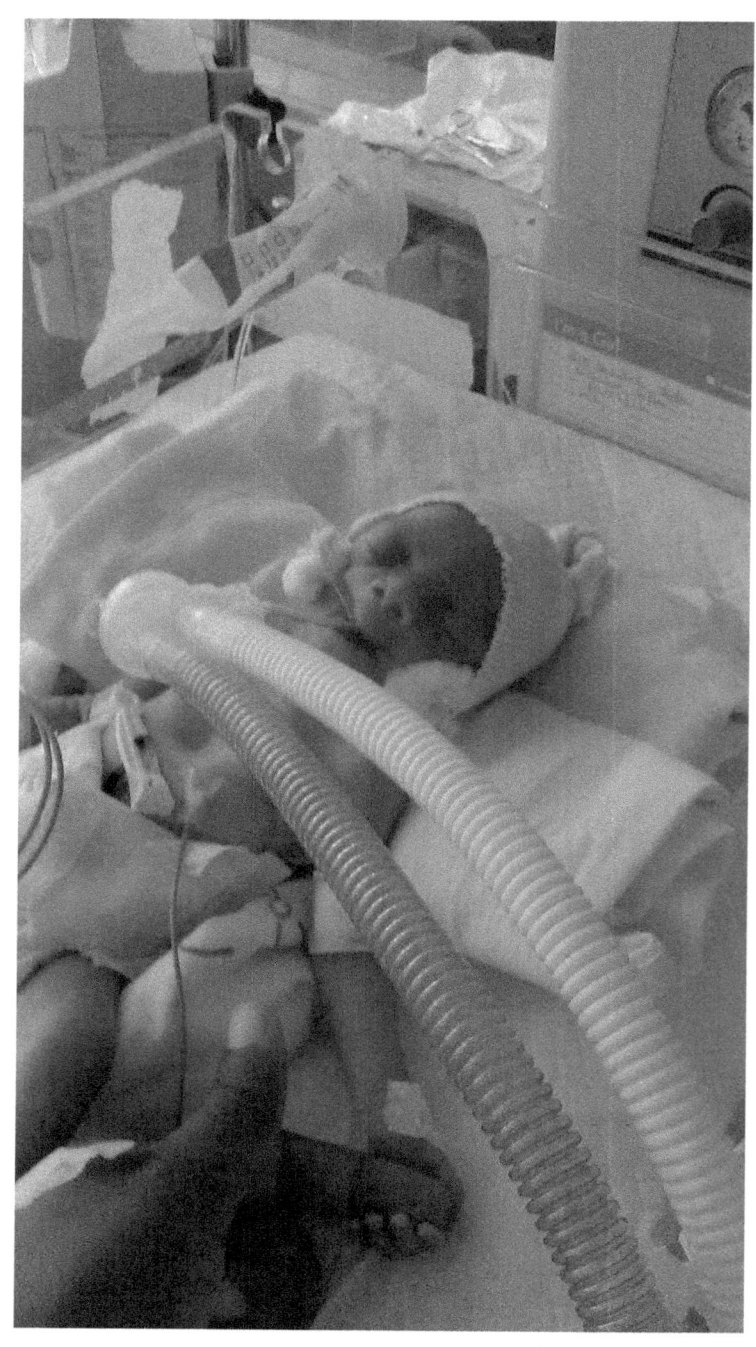

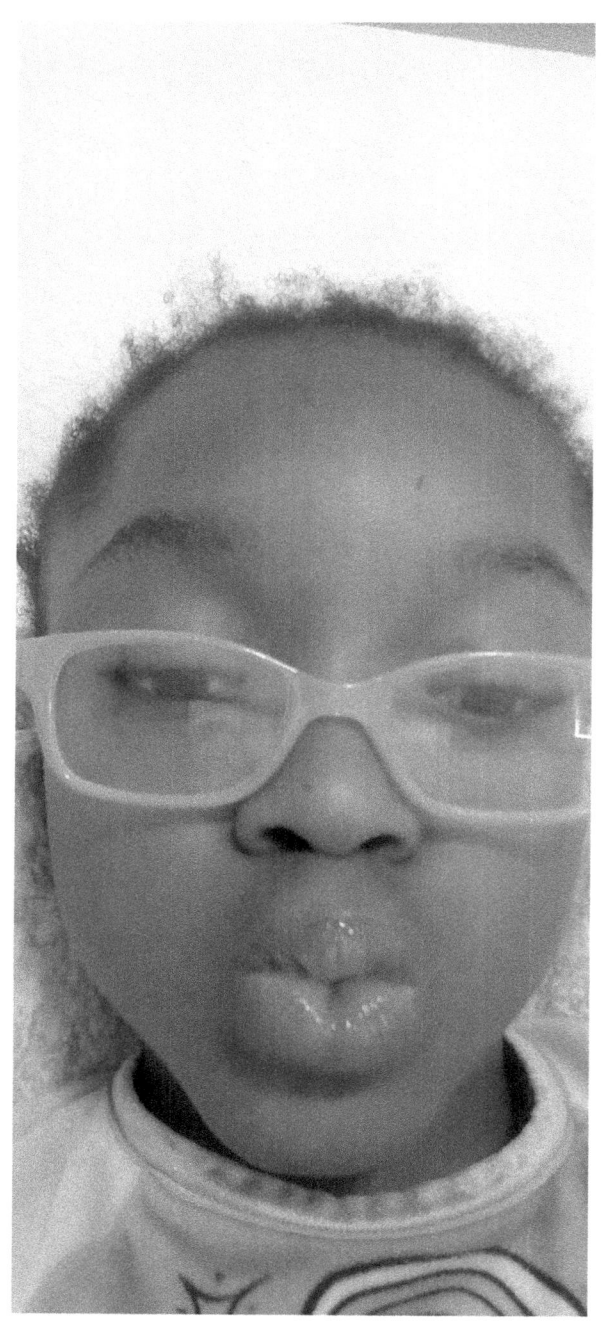

About the Author

Nicholette Goffe is a Certified Accountant who also holds a Master's Degree in Business Administration (MBA). She has built a successful career working in various accounting and senior accounting roles in Jamaica before continuing her professional journey in the United States, where she now serves as an Accounting Manager. Her expertise and dedication in the field of finance reflect her commitment to excellence and perseverance.

Beyond her professional accomplishments, Nicholette's life was forever changed by her daughter's fight for survival in the Neonatal Intensive Care Unit (NICU). Inspired by the resilience and courage she witnessed each day, she wrote Tiny Warrior: A Preemie's Fight for Life to uplift and encourage families navigating the challenges of premature birth.

Born and raised in Jamaica in a loving family with both parents and two siblings, Nicholette developed strong family values and resilience that carried her through the toughest season of her life. Throughout her daughter's NICU journey, her family became her foundation, offering unwavering support, while friends stepped in with kindness and strength when it was needed most.

Now living in Florida, Nicholette balances her career with her most cherished role—being a devoted mother. When she isn't working with numbers, she treasures every moment with her husband, and her daughter, the tiny warrior who inspired her story.